MELVIN BERGER

DATA PROCESSING

A Computer-Awareness
First Book

Franklin Watts
New York | London | Toronto
Sydney | 1983

A GROLIER COMPANY

Diagram by Vantage Art, Inc.

Photographs courtesy of
IBM: Opp. p. 1, pp. 10, 24, 34, and 51;
Wang Laboratories, Inc.: pp. 5,
11 (bottom), 14 (bottom), and 38;
United Press International: p. 6;
Texas Instruments: pp. 11 (top right and
left) and 14 (top); n.c.: p. 17;
New York Public Library Picture Collection:
p. 25 (left); ITT: pp. 25 (right) and 45;
Sidney Harris: p. 32;
United Nations: p. 37 (Saw Lwin);
Tandy Corp./Radio Shack: pp. 44 (top
and bottom) and 48 (top and bottom);
Rothco: p. 59 (Punch).

Library of Congress Cataloging in Publication Data

Berger, Melvin.
Data processing.

(A Computer-awareness first book)
Includes index.
Summary: Defines data processing and
describes the functions of computer
input and output, processing,
storage, and programming.
1. Electronic data processing—
Juvenile literature.
2. Computers—Juvenile literature.
[1. Data processing. 2. Computers]
I. Title. II. Series.
QA76.23.B473 1983 001.64 83-6879
ISBN 0-531-04640-0

Printed in the United States of America
10 9 8 7 6

CONTENTS

DATA PROCESSING

CHAPTER ONE

DATA PROCESSING: A DEFINITION

"U.S. SPACE EFFORT DEPENDS ON HIGH-SPEED DATA PROCESSING"

"DATA PROCESSING RUNS AIRLINE"

"AUTOMAKER USES DATA PROCESSING TO PLAN OUTPUT"

"DATA PROCESSING MAKES ADVANCED RESEARCH POSSIBLE"

"POLICE USE DATA PROCESSING TO CATCH KILLER"

Headlines such as these have been appearing more and more often in recent years. They make very clear the vital role that data processing plays in modern life.

But exactly what *is* data processing?

Briefly stated, it is the act of changing facts and figures into useful information.

DATA

Any definition of data processing must include first an explanation of the word *data*. *Data* is the plural form of the word *datum*.

The word *data* is treated as singular, however, whenever it refers to the collective noun "information."

Data are facts. Often, they are called *raw facts* (or *raw data*). They are raw because they are not arranged or organized in any order when put into the computer.

There are any number of different kinds of data—the sales figures of a large corporation, a student's grades in school, the speeds of the different planets through space, the number of engine parts in storage at an auto factory, the names of all major-league baseball players, the changing temperatures at the center of an active volcano, the prices of groceries at a supermarket, a list of people who have borrowed books from the library, and so on.

The data may be presented in the form of numbers, letters, or special symbols such as punctuation marks, arithmetic signs, and dollar and cent signs. Data can also be represented by any combination of numbers, letters, and symbols. Computer designers sometimes call data *alphanumerics* (letter-numbers). More often, though, they use the word *characters* to cover all the diverse forms of data.

Do you have a bank account? If so, the bank's computer contains a good deal of data about you. Some of the data characters are letters, such as your name, parts of your address, and the month of your birth. Some of the characters are numbers, such as your account number, any amounts you have deposited or withdrawn, and the final balance. A few of the characters are symbols, such as commas and periods in your address and dollar signs and decimal points in the various money amounts.

To process the data concerning your account, the bank's computer adds your deposits, subtracts your withdrawals, and calculates and adds to your account any interest that you have earned. These operations change the raw data into useful information—your balance, or how much money is left in your account.

PROCESSING

Data is changed into useful information in an operation called *processing*. Processing takes in a number of steps. Consider the case of processing your bank account.

Suppose you start the month with a balance of $100. During the month you make a deposit of $50 and a withdrawal of $30. You also earn $1 in interest.

The processing begins with the arrival of the data inside the computer—the amount of money you started with, the sum you put in, the sum you took out, and the amount of interest. Then the computer goes through the necessary calculations. It adds the opening balance and the deposit **($100 + $50 = $150)**, then subtracts the withdrawal **($150 − $30 = $120)**. Finally, it adds the interest **($120 + $1 = $121)**. The computer then prints this information on your bank statement and in the bank's records. It shows both you and the bank the balance in your account.

Simple arithmetic, though, is only part of data processing. The computer also has to have a way of receiving the data on your account. In addition, it must be able to store, or remember, your name, address, account number, and all the deposits and withdrawals you made. To process the data, it has to find all the separate bits of data and the instructions on what to do with each of them. It then has to bring the data and instructions together to do the arithmetic. And finally, it has to present the results in a form that you can understand.

Data and processing are two of the three components that make up modern data processing. The machine that brings them together is the third part—the wonder invention of the twentieth century, the *computer*.

THE COMPUTER

A computer is an electronic device that processes raw data. Given its instructions by human beings, the computer can process data at incredible speeds. A new, advanced computer can go through hundreds of millions of separate mathematical operations in one second! And it performs these entirely without error.

Yet, amazing as they are, some people call computers high-speed idiots. Surely, they are high speed. But idiots?

Computers are considered "stupid" because of the limited number of operations even the best computers can perform. Computers only "look" smart, thanks to their high speed and huge memory.

Computers can calculate. That is, they can add, subtract, multiply, and divide. Also, they can compare numbers or letters and perform logical operations. That is to say, they can compare two numbers and determine if those numbers are the same or, if not, which one is larger. When given long lists of names or words, they can put them in alphabetical order or arrange them in any way desired.

Computers can hold huge amounts of information and can locate this information quickly when instructed to do so. And computers can communicate with human beings. Through certain devices they can take in data that is fed to them, and through certain other devices they can give out information in a form that people can understand.

FORTY YEARS OF DATA PROCESSING

When you picture a computer, do you see rows of shiny cabinets with flashing lights and whirling tapes filling a large room ? Or do you think of a small, sleek, modern unit that sits atop a desk and looks like a typewriter attached to a TV screen?

Actually, both the machines just described are computers. They are alike, yet different. They work in the same basic way and can do about the same jobs. The main difference is in the speed of processing and in data-storage capacity.

WANG
INVENTORY MASTER FILE MAINTENANCE
ENTER ITEM NO.(0=END OR -1=VOID)
PROD ID. - 000000000100 TRANS - C
1 DESC No. 2 Pencils
2 ALT. ID
3 LOC CODE A3
4 PREFIX 001
5 U/M dz
6 LAST ACT. 09/04/79
7 VENDOR ID. OP100
8 ON HAND 62
9 ON ORDER 28
10 MINIMUM 90
11 MAXIMUM 125
12 AVG. COST 0.75
13 LAST COST 0.75
14 PRICE 1 0.85
15 PRICE 2 0.83
16 PRICE 3 0.80
17 WEIGHT 0.0000

COMMUNICATIONS CONTROL CENTER
CITY OF CHATTANOOGA POLICE DEPARTMENT
CH09
751-5082
POLICE
DEPARTMENT
Call Check

The computer's role in data processing has been changing. The first true electronic computer was built in 1946 at the Moore School of Electrical Engineering at the University of Pennsylvania. The inventors were Drs. John W. Mauchly and J. Presper Eckert, Jr. It was called ENIAC, an acronym for the name Electronic Numerical Integrator And Computer.

ENIAC was a one-of-kind machine. It weighed more than 30 tons and filled a room 30 by 50 feet (9 by 15 m). Inside were 18,000 vacuum tubes—bulblike devices that were used in all radios and televisions of that period. ENIAC could perform about 4,500 additions in one second.

Since that pioneering effort, the trend has been to develop smaller, faster, cheaper, and more reliable computers. Some are still about the same size as ENIAC. But they pack much more computing power, storage, and dependability into the same volume. These large computers are called *mainframes,* or *maxicomputers.*

Many large government agencies, such as those involved with the census, taxes, defense, and the space program, have mainframe computers. Mainframes are used also by large banks and other major financial institutions, large corporations, airlines, hotel chains, and car-rental firms. Large computers are also found at the headquarters of the FBI and at state and city police-department headquarters. A good number of scientific research laboratories have put mainframes to work collecting and processing vast amounts of data as well.

This Chattanooga, Tennessee, police department's sophisticated computer system is also linked to the large computer at the National Crime Information Center in Washington, D.C.

Mainframes today cost from around $500,000 to more than $10 million. Of course, this is too expensive for many users, who may at times require the powerful computing capacity of a mainframe but don't need it full time. Such users may turn to an arrangement called *time-sharing*. In time-sharing, several organizations divide the use of one large computer. A mainframe computer can serve several thousand users.

Time-sharing is possible because the computer processes data far faster than human beings can feed it new data. The computer can also give out information much faster than people can make use of that information.

Several small factories may use time-sharing on a mainframe owned by a large company. The large company actually sells time on its computer. Each second of computer time is divided into thousands of tiny parts. The various factories are assigned a certain number of time slots within each second. Every factory has a terminal that is connected by telephone lines to the central computer.

Let us say that a computer operator at Factory A enters some data—the company's most recent sales figures—into the computer. The operator wants to know if there is enough demand to justify an increase in production. The computer gives this information in a fraction of a second. The operator is not even aware that dozens of others are using the computer for their own purposes at almost exactly the same time. Each user feels in sole charge of the computer.

Despite its many uses, the mainframe computer is not suitable for everyone. In 1965, Digital Equipment Corporation introduced a smaller computer.

Diminished in size, with less storage capacity and slower processing capabilities, this computer came to be called a *minicomputer*. The minicomputer appealed mainly to laboratory scientists and engineers—people who had no great need for the power of the larger computers but required a machine that would perform complex numerical calculations rapidly.

Soon, though, businesses and other users began to clamor for minicomputers, too. Manufacturers offered machines that served new and varied applications. Separate units, called *hang-ons, add-ons,* or *peripherals,* were built that could be attached to minicomputers. The attachments added to the unit's input and output options and to its storage capacity. As technology advanced, the minicomputers came ever closer to the mainframes in performance. The price, though, was much lower, from $10,000 to $250,000.

Minicomputers were not the last word in computers, either. In short order they were joined by the even smaller *microcomputers.* A typical microcomputer sits on top of a desk.

The microcomputer was made possible by the revolution in microelectronics of the last decades. ENIAC's thousands of vacuum tubes, which once filled a large room, were replaced by 64,000 or more electronic elements on a silicon wafer chip no bigger than the nail of your little finger. With the silicon chip, microcomputers can do more calculating faster and better than ENIAC did. The typical microcomputer is about two-millionths the size of ENIAC.

Microcomputers are also known as *small, home,* or *personal computers.* They serve a wide variety of data-processing purposes. These same machines also have many other applications, from playing games and teaching school subjects to composing music and figuring out taxes. Most microcomputers cost between $100 and $10,000.

Microelectronics and the many add-ons that are available have made microcomputers suitable for all but the most advanced and largest computer applications. And since the mid-1970s, the so-called *superminis* that have come on the market compete directly with mainframe computers.

Above: ENIAC was the first true electronic computer. *Facing page:* the tiny microprocessor chip was primarily responsible for the development of microcomputers such as the Wang Professional Computer and the Texas Instruments' TI-99/4a home computer.

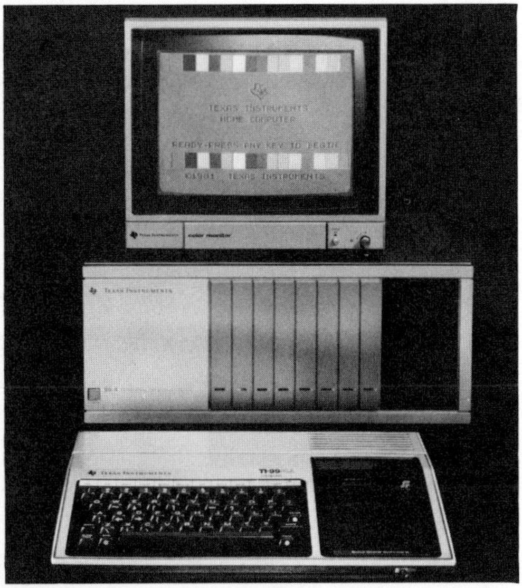
TEXAS INSTRUMENTS
HOME COMPUTER
READY-PRESS ANY KEY TO BEGIN
©1981 TEXAS INSTRUMENTS
TEXAS INSTRUMENTS

WANG

The superminis cost less than half the price of a mainframe computer. They can be used for time-sharing, and for many commercial and scientific purposes. With add-ons, most superminis can come close to duplicating the processing capabilities and information storage of even the largest mainframes. In time, they may replace most of the largest computers. Mainframes will be used only for such applications as checking federal income-tax returns, long-range weather forecasting, and so on.

The next time you are in a bank, supermarket, or government office, ask about its computer. Find out if it is a mainframe, supermini, minicomputer, or microcomputer. See if you can learn which kind of computer handles the data processing of your school grades, your parents' paychecks, and the family telephone bill.

CHAPTER TWO

COMPUTER INPUT

Computers, we know, come in various sizes and shapes. Yet, different as they are, all computers have a number of almost identical parts.

Basic to every computer are four parts we touched on earlier: an *input device*, a *central processing unit*, *storage* or *memory*, and an *output device*. Together these make up what is called the *hardware*, or machinery, of the computer.

The other necessary part of computer operation is the *software*. This consists of a list of instructions, or *program*, that directs the operation of the hardware.

Human beings, as well as machines other than computers, communicate with a computer by means of an input device. An input device takes in data in the form of words, numbers, and characters and changes that data into a code that the computer can understand.

Most modern input devices make this changeover automatically. The human operator feeds the data into the machine. The computer itself then puts that data into machine-readable form.

COMPUTER TERMINAL

The most common way to enter data into a computer is by means of a typewriter-like device called a *keyboard*. An operator types

Keyboards, such as this one from Texas Instruments *(above)*, are input devices. The video display screen *(right)* shows the user what he or she has typed in—the software program—and the results of the processing.

the words and numbers on the keyboard, and they automatically pass into the computer. An attached TV monitor, or *video display screen,* shows what the operator is typing. The keyboard and video display screen together make up what is usually referred to as the *computer terminal.*

The screen allows the worker to catch any error before it affects the entire computer operation. If there is something wrong, the operator can edit out the trouble spot and replace it with the correct data. The same screen can also be used to display the results of the processing, or output.

Here is a typical instance of using the screen to catch an error: An airline reservation clerk is entering information into a computer terminal concerning a roundtrip flight from New York to Los Angeles and back. He keys in the date of departure as June 20, 1983. By mistake, the clerk punches in a return flight on the same day. A glance at the screen shows him the mistake. The operator then makes the correction and changes the return date to July 20, 1983.

Quite often, the computer itself is able to pick up obvious mistakes made in input. For example, once, while entering a department-store customer's address, a computer operator keyed in the zip code as 170E4. The program had been instructed that all zip codes would have five digits and no letters. Immediately a bell rang, and the words **NOT CORRECT** appeared on the screen. The operator checked and found that the number should have been 17034. The input was then easily edited, and the correct number was entered.

Some terminals that are connected to distant computers have no computing ability of their own. These are known as *dumb terminals,* and their only use is to feed data into a central computer and get information back from that computer. The other type of terminals are the so-called *smart terminals.* These terminals not only communicate with a larger computer but also are able to do some of their own computing.

Typing at a terminal is but one of several ways of entering data into a computer. One method sometimes still used is the *punched card.*

PUNCHED CARDS

Punched cards are rectangular in shape, about 7 3/8 by 3 1/4 inches (18.4 by 8.3 cm). Made of stiff paper, when in use they have small holes punched in them. Sometimes they are called *IBM cards,* because IBM was the first company to use them.

Data is entered on the punched cards by means of a *keypunch* machine. The keypunch machine has a keyboard and attached mechanisms that make a different pattern of holes for each character on the keyboard.

A punched card usually has the numbers 0 to 9 printed in ten rows across it. There are eighty separate columns of these numbers. Each column can contain just one character, one single unit of data.

Numbers are represented by holes punched through that digit on the card. To enter the number 3, for instance, a small, rectangular hole is punched through the number 3 in one of the columns. Letters are shown by a hole above the printed numbers plus a hole through one of the digits. Symbols are indicated by different combinations of holes above and through the digits.

After the data is entered onto the punched card, it must still pass into the computer. This is accomplished by means of an input device called a *card reader.* The computer operator puts a stack of punched cards into the input hopper. The machine then pulls out one card at a time to be read.

The card is read in one of two ways. In a certain type of reader, the card is whirled around a metal roller that has eighty or ninety-six narrow metal brushes resting against it. Where there is a hole, a brush touches the roller, thereby closing an electrical circuit. In this fashion, each hole is sensed, and the card is thus read.

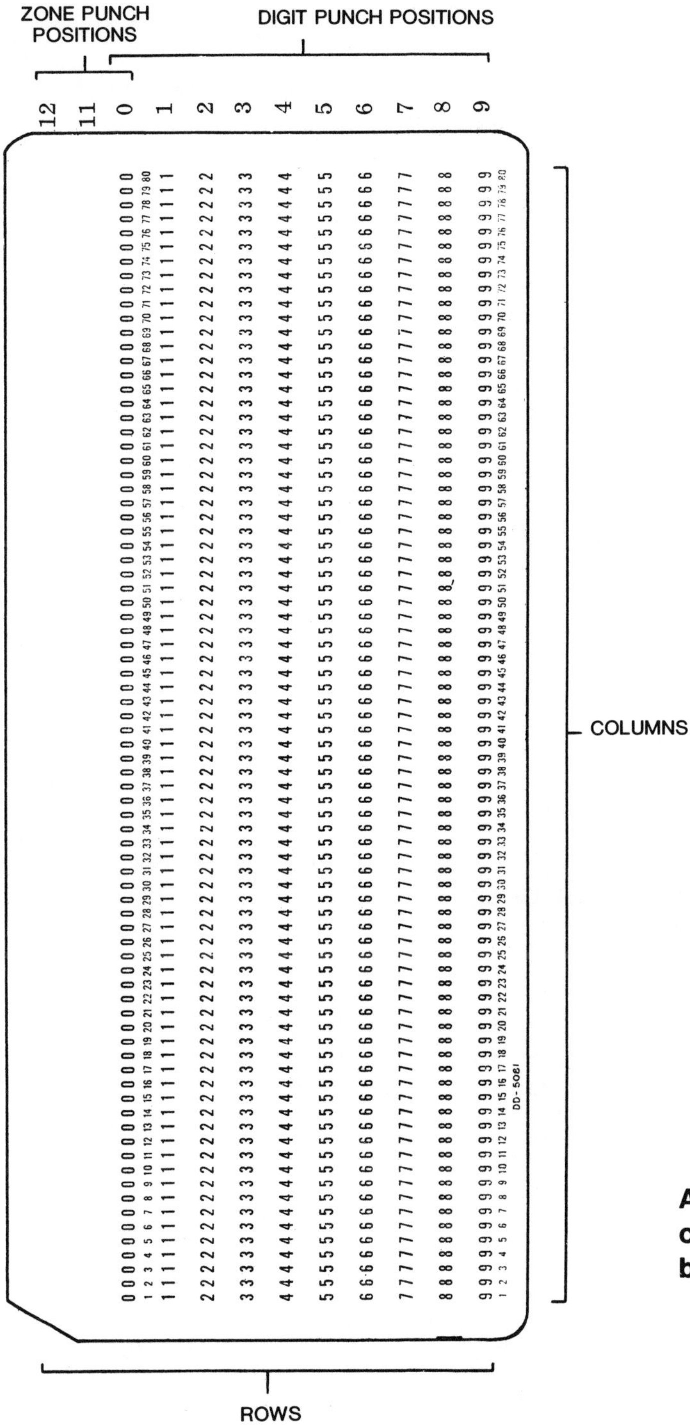

A punched card before being coded

The other approach to reading the card involves using light. The card is passed between a light source and a number of tiny photoelectric cells. Each cell produces a small electrical current when it is struck by light. Therefore, each time there is an opening over a photoelectric cell, light strikes the cell, electricity flows, and the pattern of holes is read.

KEY-TO-DISK AND KEY-TO-TAPE

Two input devices that are much faster and more advanced than the punched card are known as the *key-to-disk* and *key-to-tape.* As in keypunch, to use either of these instruments, the operator must sit at a keyboard and type in the data.

In both key-to-disk and key-to-tape, the data is entered as tiny magnetic spots. However, key-to-disk enters these spots on a flat disk, similar to a phonograph record, while key-to-tape enters them on a long roll of tape resembling that used in tape recorders. Just as the holes on the punched card are a code for the data to be entered into the computer, so the magnetic spots on the disk or tape are a code for the data, too. (Magnetic disk and magnetic tape are discussed more fully in Chapter Four.)

UNIVERSAL PRODUCT CODE

Supermarket managers have many needs for data processing. They need to know how well each item is selling, when to order more stock, how many units have been sold at sale prices, ways to speed up checkout lines, and so on. To accomplish these goals, almost every product sold in supermarkets has a rectangular patch of zebralike stripes printed on the package, can, or jar label. This is called the *Universal Product Code*. The data it contains appears in the form of thick and thin vertical bars with printed numbers underneath. The first five digits of the Universal Product Code indicate the manufacturer's code number. The second five refer to a particular product's code number.

The supermarket checkout clerk slides the item, with the Universal Product Code facing down, over an opening in the counter. Inside is an input device—a laser light source that "reads" the bars. The numbers of the manufacturer and product go to a central computer, which searches its memory for the price of the item. In a flash, the price appears on a screen and on the cash register's paper tape. At the same time, the computer makes a record of the sale. Later, the computer processes this data and displays the figures for the store manager to examine.

MICR

Every day, the banks of the world have the staggering task of handling billions of checks. This task has been made much easier with the help of computers and data processing.

Have you ever noticed the string of strangely shaped numbers printed across the bottom of all canceled bank checks? They are part of the check's *Magnetic Ink Character Recognition,* or *MICR.* The numbers are printed with a special magnetic ink. The first group of numbers identifies the bank; the second group gives the specific amount of the check.

Suppose someone writes a check for $36 and uses it to pay for theater tickets. The box-office worker deposits the check in the theater's bank account. The bank next sends the check to the customer's bank to collect the money. There, a computer operator keys in the written amount of the check, $36. These numbers appear, without the dollar sign or decimal point, following the printed numbers. You can see them under the customer's signature. Look at some canceled checks, and see if the final numbers in the MICR line are the same as the written-in amount.

Then the check is placed in an MICR reader. At high speed the check spins around a thick metal post that is an input device.

The post "senses" magnetic letters identifying the bank, the account number, and the amount. This data is entered into the computer. The money is withdrawn from the checkwriter's account and deposited in the theater account. Modern MICR readers can handle almost 3,000 checks a minute in this way.

OCR

The limitations of MICR are that the characters must be printed with special magnetic ink and that only one line of text can be read from each document. *Optical Character Recognition,* or *OCR,* improves on this system.

With an OCR reader, the computer can read any words or numbers that are printed, typed, or written neatly by hand. The computer memory has been fed the shape of each of the letters and numbers beforehand. Then, whenever it "senses" that particular shape, it knows it to be that specific character.

Some electric-utility companies use OCR for processing the checks they receive from their customers. The customers are instructed to send back a stub of the bill with their payment. The stub has such vital bits of information as the date, the customer's account number, and the amount due.

A data-entry operator enters the amount of the check in special boxes on the bill stub. An OCR reader then reads the information on the stub and the amount of money that was paid. The computer compares the two figures and indicates whether the amount is correct or not, and if not, whether it is too much or too little.

One big problem with OCR readers is that they cannot deal with misspellings or sloppy writing. If an auto manufacturer gets an order for a 60-cylinder car, a human clerk knows at once that it is a mistake and changes it to 6 cylinders. The OCR reader, however, senses it as 60 cylinders, and the computer might break down trying to direct the building of a car that size. In one new

OCR input device, when the machine cannot understand a character, it displays that letter or number on a screen. This gets the attention of a human operator, who notices the mistake and keys in the correct character.

VOICE RECOGNITION

In recent years, voice-recognition computer input devices have become available. These are equipped to receive data in the form of spoken words or commands. Instead of keying in data, the operator has only to speak, and the computer changes the figures or words into machine language.

Today, voice-recognition input devices are limited to perhaps a few hundred different words and numbers. But researchers are working to develop machines that can respond to whole sentences or to complicated instructions. And chances are that in the years to come, scientists will invent even better and more useful input devices, devices that are not even dreamed of today!

CHAPTER THREE

COMPUTER PROCESSING

At the heart of every computer is the central processing unit, which is usually abbreviated as *CPU*. It takes its name, *central*, from the fact that all parts of the computer—the input device, output device, and any outside memory storage—are all attached to it. And it is called *processing unit* because it is here that most of the computer's actual work, the calculating and changing of the data, takes place.

THE CPU

When it comes to processing the data, the CPU plays a number of important roles. First, it is a traffic cop. That is to say, it controls and directs all the operations within the computer. It locates the data in storage and the instructions needed to solve a problem, brings them together, starts and stops the processing routine, and tells the different components what to do and when to do it.

The CPU is also a mathematician. It can solve the most complex problems with great ease and near-perfect accuracy. The fantastic mathematical ability of the CPU does not come from its having a great number of different skills. It can perform only the simple actions of adding, subtracting, multiplying, and dividing. Its extraordinary power comes from the way it is able to combine these operations and its unfailing accuracy and speed. In minutes, a computer works out a math problem that would take hundreds of experts, all working together, several days or weeks to solve.

In addition, the CPU is a logician. This means that it makes decisions based on logic, decisions that mostly involve comparing two different values or characters to see whether they are the same or different. If they are different, the CPU tells which is bigger and which is smaller. Also, it determines which value comes first, in any order desired. Finally, once a decision is made, the CPU decides—on the basis of the previous decision—what the next step should be.

In the early days of computers, the CPU was built around racks of large vacuum tubes. In later computers, vacuum tubes were replaced by transistors and semiconductors. These served the same functions as vacuum tubes but took up only a tiny fraction of the space.

Modern CPUs use *microprocessors.* These small chips of silicon, about the size of a fingernail, have the semiconductors built into them. Working on a microscopic scale, scientists and engineers add impurities to the silicon to create the semiconductors. The electrical circuits are actually etched right onto the microprocessor's surface. As a result, electronic components that once required thousands of tubes and miles of wire are now placed on a chip that is no more than 1/4-inch (0.6-cm) square.

Microprocessors made the microcomputer possible. But they are widely used in large computers as well. It is improved microprocessors that have let mainframe computers, minicomputers, and microcomputers squeeze ever more computing power and memory into ever smaller spaces.

MATH FUNCTION

The electronic circuits and semiconductor switches on the microprocessor perform the part of data processing that deals with numbers and arithmetic.

01751
LOCATION
P
DATE OUT
DATE IN

Facing page: early computer "brains" were built around large racks of vacuum tubes. *Above left:* a microprocessor chip enlarged 50 times. This chip can perform more than 300,000 logical operations a second. *Right:* using a light board and a greatly enlarged picture of a microprocessor chip, the engineer in this picture is able to design integrated circuits that will later be etched right onto the silicon chip's surface.

Suppose you are the manager of a baseball team. You can use your home computer to process many kinds of statistical information about your players.

You might want to calculate each player's batting average, for example. A batting average is found by dividing the number of hits by the number of times at bat. You start by programming your computer to follow a specific sequence of steps with the data you will be entering.

On the keyboard of your computer you enter the first player's name, the number of hits (6), and the number of times at bat (24). The computer, or more exactly the CPU, goes through the steps of the program. It divides the hits (6) by the times at bat (24) and finds that the first player's batting average is .250.

You enter the data for each of the other players in the same way, and run it through the computer. The computer comes up with each player's batting average. Because the computer program also includes instructions on how to present the results in a form you can read, the video display screen on command will show you each player's name and batting average.

You may also instruct the computer to store the information in its memory. This will enable you to see how each team member's batting average changes during the season.

Can you think of other math operations that would help a baseball manager? a track coach? a swimming coach?

LOGIC FUNCTION

The logic system of the CPU can do various kinds of comparisons. It can then undertake other operations based on the results of these comparisons.

There are three common forms of comparison. These are: to determine if two values are equal, to determine if one value is smaller than another, and to determine if one value is greater than another. Here, now, are some examples of the kinds of comparisons performed by computers.

One college requires that its students maintain a straight A average in order to be named an honor student. Its computer compares each of the students' letter grades with the standard A. If all of the letter grades of a student are the same, that person's name is printed on the honor list. If any of the grade letters are different, that name is not printed.

A large city gives a written test for all men and women who want to become police officers. City officials have decided that only candidates who get fewer than twenty-seven wrong answers on the test will be appointed to the force. The several hundred test scores are entered into the computer. The instructions in the program are to compare the number wrong on the test score with the number 27 and to select only those test scores that are lower. The computer then prints a list of those candidates whose total of wrong answers is below 27.

A mail-order book distributor has a computer on the lookout for large orders. Company policy offers one free book for every order over $15. All the orders are processed through the firm's computer. At one point, each order is compared with the value of 15 in the computer's CPU. If the order amount proves to be greater than 15, the computer printout shows that the customer should receive the gift book.

Finally, every fall, about 20,000 students register at a big state university. For their records, the university officials need an alphabetical list of all the students. The university instructs its computer to read the names and arrange them in this special order. The CPU quickly moves them about and within just a few minutes prints out a list of all the students, A through Z.

THE BINARY SYSTEM

The computer is an electronic machine; this means that it runs on electricity. Electricity is usually thought of as existing in two states—off (not flowing) or on (flowing). Machine language, which is the language of the computer, uses only two symbols—

off and on (though low power and high power are occasionally used instead). The most common form these two symbols take are the digits 0 and 1, representing, respectively, off and on.

The mathematical system that uses only two digits is called the *binary system.* The internal workings of all computers are based on this number system. Every character of data can be represented by some combination of zeros and ones.

The basic unit of data in the computer is the *bit* (made up from the first two letters and last letter of the words binary digit). Each bit, then, is either a zero (0) or a one (1), off or on.

Some computers use a group of four bits to represent numbers. Each bit has a different value. The fourth bit, the one at the end, has a value of one. The binary number 0001, therefore, equals one in the decimal system. The third bit, next to the end, is twice as big, or two. Thus, 0010 equals two in decimal. The second bit is double that, so 0100 is equal to four. And the first place has the value of eight; 1000 equals eight.

When a bit shows a zero, it adds nothing to the number. But each one adds one, two, four, or eight, depending on its position.

Here is how to count from zero to decimal nine in binary numbers:

Decimal	*Binary*
0	0000
1	0001
2	0010
3	0011
4	0100
5	0101
6	0110
7	0111
8	1000
9	1001

One group of four bits is limited. It cannot represent all the numbers, letters, and symbols that are required. Therefore, many computers also use a second set of four bits. The original four bits are called the *digit*. The additional four bits, which come before the digit, are known as the *zone*.

The eight bits of the zone and digit make up a *byte*. Within a computer, each character is represented by a single byte. With the zone and digit, it is possible to depict all the characters that may be necessary. To represent the individual digits, for example, the zone contains four ones:

Decimal	*Zone/Digit*
1	1111/0001
6	1111/0110

The first nine letters of the alphabet (A through I) are shown this way:

Letter	*Zone/Digit*
A	1100/0001
B	1100/0010
C	1100/0011
D	1100/0100
E	1100/0101
F	1100/0110
G	1100/0111
H	1100/1000
I	1100/1001

In words, these letters are shown by 1100 in the zone, and the count goes from decimal one to decimal nine in the digit. For the next nine letters (J through R), the zone is 1101, and the digit again runs from one to nine. For the final eight letters (S through

Z), the zone is 1110, and the digit goes from two to nine. Various combinations of zeros and ones in both the zone and digit are used for the symbols.

Using the binary system in our daily lives would be slow and awkward. Instead of writing the zip code on a letter as 13059, in the computer binary code we would have to write 1111/0001 1111/0011 1111/0000 1111/0101 1111/1001.

The computer must use this system, since it can only handle zeros and ones (power off and power on). Because of its remarkable speed, though, it can write numbers and solve problems using the binary system much, much faster than you could using the common decimal system.

Although the computer must operate on a system based on the binary code, human beings using the computer can present data to it in the form of decimal numbers and ordinary words. This is because the computer contains a built-in program that translates these numbers and words into binary code. Then, when the processing is completed, the same computer program translates the binary results back into decimal numbers and words that are familiar to human beings. (For more information on computer languages, see Chapter Six.)

CHAPTER FOUR

COMPUTER STORAGE

Computer storage is the place within the computer where data and instructions are stored until they are needed. (It is *not* a warehouse where the machines are kept until they are ready to be used!) Computer storage is often called *memory.*

Several types of information are stored in a computer's memory. The computer holds the raw data that it is fed. It also stores the instructions, or program, necessary to process the data. And finally, it retains the results of the processing.

Because there can be so much data to be remembered, many computers have two storage areas. One is within the CPU. Usually, the program and the data being acted upon are kept there. This is called the computer's *main storage.*

There is often another, separate storage section. Data reserved for later use is deposited there. This unit is known as the computer's *auxiliary,* or *secondary, storage.*

MAIN STORAGE

Many units of data, or bytes (characters), can be stored in a computer's memory. The main storage of a microcomputer may hold just over 64,000 bytes. This figure though, is usually written as 64K. The K stands for *kilo,* the Greek word for "thousand." In

"SURE IT'S DEPRESSING. THIS THING HAS A MEMORY OF 3 TRILLION BITS, AND I CAN'T RECALL WHAT I HAD FOR LUNCH."

computer use, K is actually slightly higher. It equals 1,024, which comes from the binary system (two times itself ten times). The 64K is equal to exactly 65,536 bytes. Newer, more advanced computers are able to hold many millions of bytes!

With room for such immense numbers of bytes in its memory, it is clear that the computer has to have a fast, sure way to locate each one. This is why each byte is assigned a specific *address* in the computer's storage.

A computer address is a number. It is given to only one byte, and it specifies that byte's exact location in memory. Just like the street number in your address tells exactly where you live, so the number of the data's address tells the computer just where the data is to be found.

To retrieve data, the computer must often know how many characters make up a complete unit. Such a unit of data, or group of characters, is called a *field*.

It is well known that many records include a person's Social Security number. All Social Security numbers contain nine digits or, put another way, have a field of nine characters. The address for a Social Security number, therefore, must specify both the address of the first character, which might be a number such as 8040, and the nine-character length of the field.

Over the years, computer manufacturers have hit on many different ways to store data. At first, they used electrical circuits that contained vacuum tubes. The main drawback of this method was that the tubes were large and bulky. What's more, the tubes consumed a good deal of electricity, created a lot of heat that had to be removed, were costly, lasted only a very short time, and were not completely reliable.

In the 1950s, computer manufacturers began replacing vacuum tubes with magnetic-core storage. Tiny doughnut-shaped pieces of metal were strung on a crisscross grid of very thin wires. Each piece of metal, or core, was about half the size of this letter o.

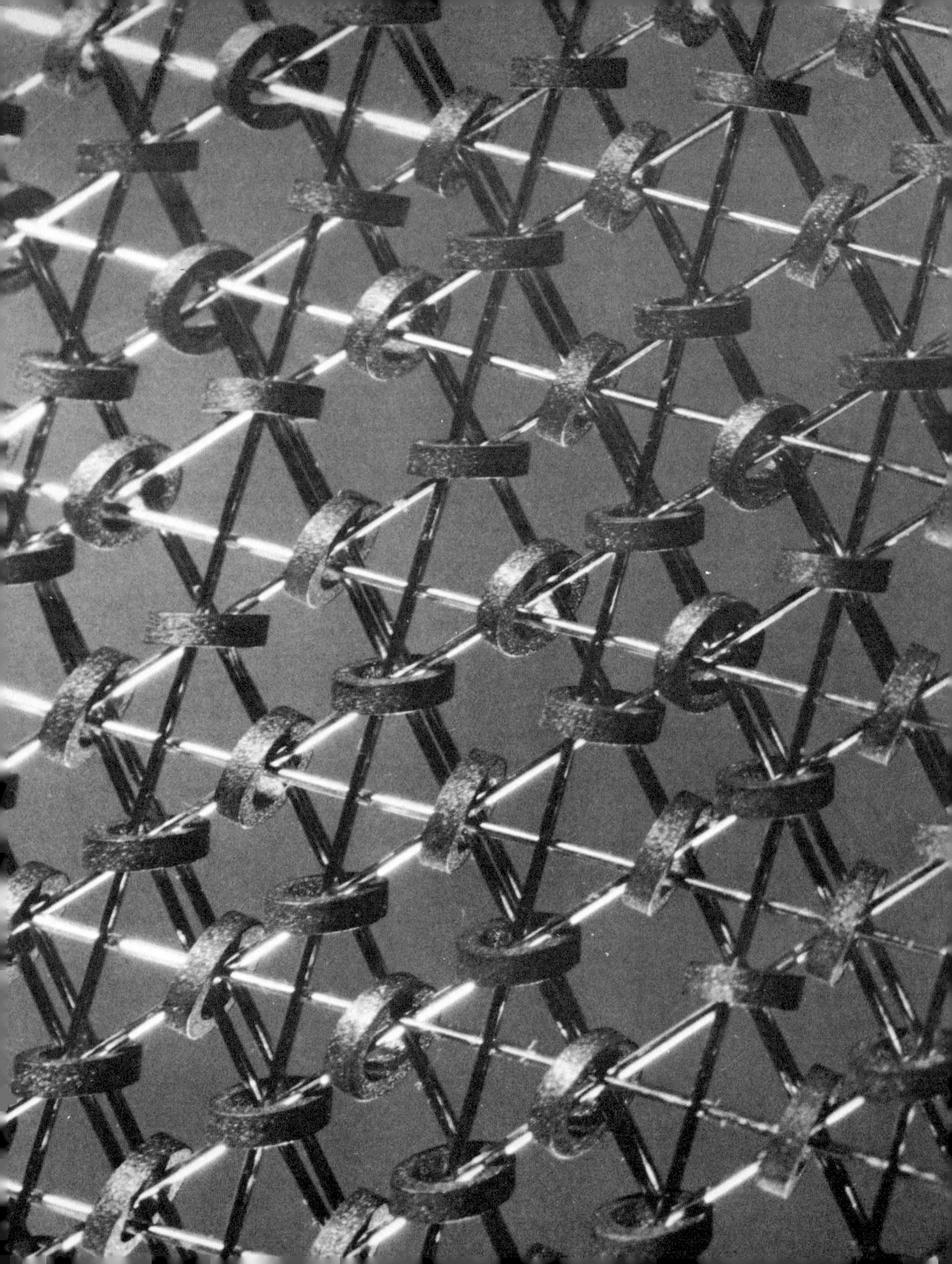

The individual cores were magnetized by a current that flowed through the wires on which they were strung. When the current flowed in one direction, the core was magnetized in that direction. When the current was reversed, the magnetism went in the opposite direction. Thus, each core could be magnetized in one direction only. The magnetism of each core could be read by another wire that was threaded through the core. The two directions of the magnetism corresponded to the two digits, 0 and 1, of the binary system.

Magnetic-core storage had several advantages over the vacuum tubes. The cores were tiny, used little energy, produced no heat, cost much less, lasted forever, and were dependable in their performance.

Then, around 1960, small electronic devices called transistors were invented. They, too, could be used instead of vacuum tubes. With transistors, computers became smaller and even more reliable.

A decade later came a further improvement—miniature semiconductor memory devices made of tiny chips of silicon. Since thousands of semiconductors and their circuits are integrated on a single unit, the chip is often called an LSI, short for Large-Scale Integrated memory chip.

The LSIs surpass the older devices in many ways. Microscopic in size, they are cheap, energy-efficient, nearly indestructible, and very reliable. Most astounding is their operating speed. Data from a magnetic-core memory could be read in millionths of a second. Yet this is slow in comparison with LSI memory chips, which measure their speed of operation in billionths of a second.

Magnetic cores on wires

AUXILIARY STORAGE

Banks keep permanent computer records of every transaction. Many schools keep computer files on every student, including his or her classes, teachers, and grades, until long after the student graduates. Every ten years, the United States government takes a census and compiles the data drawn from more than 200 million Americans.

Even the world's largest computer does not have enough capacity in its main memory for storing such vast amounts of data for long periods of time. Nor is there any need to clutter up the computer with this data; much of it is recalled rarely, if at all. For these reasons, almost every computer system has an auxiliary, or secondary, storage capacity in addition to its main storage.

The two usual methods of storing data in auxiliary memory involve the use of *magnetic tapes* and *magnetic disks.* In both, the data is stored as tiny magnetized spots on the tape or disk surface. The approach can be compared to a musical recording. Music can be preserved as magnetized spots on recording tape or as wiggly grooves cut into the surface of a phonograph record. Both the computer data and the musical sounds can then be called up out of storage whenever desired.

The magnetic tape for computer use is usually ½ inch (1.3 cm) wide and 600, 1,200, or 2,400 feet (180, 360, or 720 m) long. Made of mylar and covered with a metal oxide, the tape can be magnetized to store data. In most computers, the magnetized spots are placed in nine rows, or channels, along its length, with each inch (2.5 cm) containing as many as 6,250.

A standard code of tiny on or off magnetized spots is used to represent each of the characters of data. The data is entered, or written, on the tape by a read/write head that is very much like the one used in sound tape recording. The data is recalled, or read, by passing the tape over the same or a different read/write head. The computer unit that passes the tape over the head, both for writing and reading data, is called a *tape drive.*

Much of the computer work done by the New York Computing Centre, which serves various departments and offices of the United Nations, is stored on magnetic tape.

A Wang magnetic disk office system.
The disks in this photograph are
inside the tape drive (left foreground).

Data is usually put on the tape in the order in which it is given. Usually a blank space, called an *interblock gap,* separates bits of data.

The fact that data is stored on tape in order, or in sequence, creates problems for certain users. Consider, for example, what it means to a computer airline reservation system. Each time ticket clerks want to find out if a seat is available on a particular flight, they have to call up the record of seat sales on that plane. There may be seat listings for thousands of different flights on one tape. It could take a very long time for the computer to read through the entire tape to find the specific flight wanted.

What was needed was auxiliary storage that would provide faster access to information. In the mid-1950s, computer designers came up with the idea of the magnetic disk, or platter.

The typical disk in use today is made of aluminum and is 14 inches (35.6 cm) in diameter. It can be a single separate disk, but more often it comes in a "pack" of five to twelve disks. The pack looks like a pile of phonograph records with small spaces between the individual records. The smooth surface of each disk is covered with magnetic material, much like the material on the surface of magnetic tape.

The single disk or disk pack is mounted on a central spindle that turns at speeds of up to 3,600 revolutions per minute (rpm). (Compare this with a long-playing phonograph record, which spins at 33⅓ rpm!) Over and under each disk is the so-called *access arm,* which contains the read/write head or heads. This head magnetizes the spots on the disk. It is also able to sense these spots to recall the data. Even though the disk is absolutely smooth, without the grooves of sound records, there are as many as 800 circular tracks for the spots to be placed along. Many millions of bytes, therefore, can be squeezed onto a single, two-sided disk.

The computer also divides the surface of the disk into a number of separate wedges, or pie-shaped areas, known as *sectors.* A typical disk may have forty individual sectors. Each sector can hold a certain number of bits. To read particular data, the computer programmer has to indicate the sector number where the data is stored.

It is possible to read out data from the disk in a tiny fraction of a second. This is because the access arm can move directly to the data, without reading through the entire disk. In addition, the arm does not touch the disk and can thus move very quickly to the proper sector. And finally, the disk is spinning at such a high speed that many revolutions occur in a very short time.

Full-sized tapes and disks are used for auxiliary storage in large computers. For micro- and minicomputers, smaller versions are sometimes preferred. Instead of regular reels of tape, there are tape cassettes and cartridges. Also, 8-inch and 5¼-inch (20.3-cm and 13.3-cm) disks, known as *diskettes,* are often chosen instead of the 14-inch (35.6-cm) disks used in the very large computers.

The diskettes look very much like 45-rpm phonograph records (see photograph opposite page 1), though they are usually kept permanently in square paper envelopes. Since many of them have their magnetic material on a flexible base, they are also called *floppy disks.* Occasionally, a large computer system will use both regular disks and floppy disks as well.

From vacuum tubes to LSI memory chips and magnetic tapes and disks—computer design has surely come a long, long way!

CHAPTER FIVE

COMPUTER OUTPUT

The season attendance figures at major-league baseball games, average grades on the national college entrance exams, the number of stereo sets sold monthly, the total number of Americans earning more than a million dollars a year—these are some of the end products of computer data processing. To deliver this information in a form that human beings can understand and use is the job of the computer's output device.

From its earliest days right up to today, the end result of computer data processing has been the printed report. You may have seen the endless strips of folded, green-barred paper that pour forth from computers. But did you know that telephone and electric bills, payroll checks, and bankbooks are also computer-produced printed reports? All these types of reports come from output devices known as *printers.*

SERIAL AND LINE PRINTERS

Printers come in assorted sizes and shapes. One of the most important features of a printer is its speed of operation. This speed is determined, in part, by whether the printer operates by the serial or line method.

Serial printers produce the characters one after another. A

fast serial printer can run up to about 350 characters per second. (Compare this with high-speed typists who can barely type that many characters per *minute*!)

Some dentists use serial printers with a micro- or minicomputer. Every month the dentists send out reminders to different patients, telling them it is time for their twice-yearly checkups. Most of the letter stays the same. All that is changed is the patient's name, address, and date.

The secretary types the personal information on a letterhead in the typewriter-like serial printer that is connected to the computer. By hitting another key, the computer itself types out the repeated, standard part of the letter. This use of a computer is referred to as *word processing*.

Banks, insurance companies, most large corporations, and many other types of computer users cannot manage with the limited speed of a serial printer, however. Their reports may contain hundreds of thousands or even millions of lines of text. It would take far too long to produce a complete report or list with a serial printer.

For these high-volume users, a line printer is necessary. A line printer can turn out an entire line of 80 or 132 characters in just one stroke.

The speed of line printers is quite remarkable. The fastest ones operate at more than 20,000 lines a minute. Advanced models are now available that print an entire page at once. Their speed is about 44,000 lines per minute!

Printers are not classified only by speed, however. They are also grouped according to the way they print the characters on the paper.

IMPACT PRINTERS

Impact printers place the image on paper by means of a striking mechanism. Such devices work on the same principle as a typewriter. A raised metal letter strikes a ribbon against the paper, imprinting the letter. The important difference, of course, is that the typewriter is operated by a human typist, while the impact printer is driven by a computer.

Impact printers are of two basic kinds: front-striking and hammer-striking. The front-striking printer most resembles a typewriter in the way it operates. A raised metal image of the character hits a ribbon against the paper. In the hammer-striking printer, a flat metal hammer pushes the paper and ribbon against the raised character.

Impact printers can produce solid characters, such as you see in ordinary printed or typewritten material. They can also produce characters made up of series of dots, called *dot matrix.*

In general, the dot-matrix characters are not as easy to read as solid characters. But dot-matrix printers are usually cheaper than the solid-character variety. That makes the choice of printer, then, largely a matter of the user's particular needs and the money available.

Of the solid-character impact printers in use today, there are four main types: daisy wheel, drum, chain, and band.

The daisy wheel gets its name from the many spokes, up to 192, that radiate out from a central hub. The spokes look something like the petals of a flower. At the end of each spoke is the raised shape of the character.

The daisy wheel is a serial, front-striking printer. In front of the characters are the ribbon and paper. Behind the characters is a hammer. As the processed information comes from the CPU, the daisy wheel spins until the right character is in position. At that instant, the hammer is tripped. This forces the character against the ribbon, imprinting it on the paper.

The advantage of the daisy wheel is that it turns out work of very high quality, just like a fine typewriter. Most word processors use daisy wheels. The chief drawback of the daisy wheel is its slowness. With a top speed of about 55 characters per second, it is quite slow as compared to other solid-character printers. It is also very noisy.

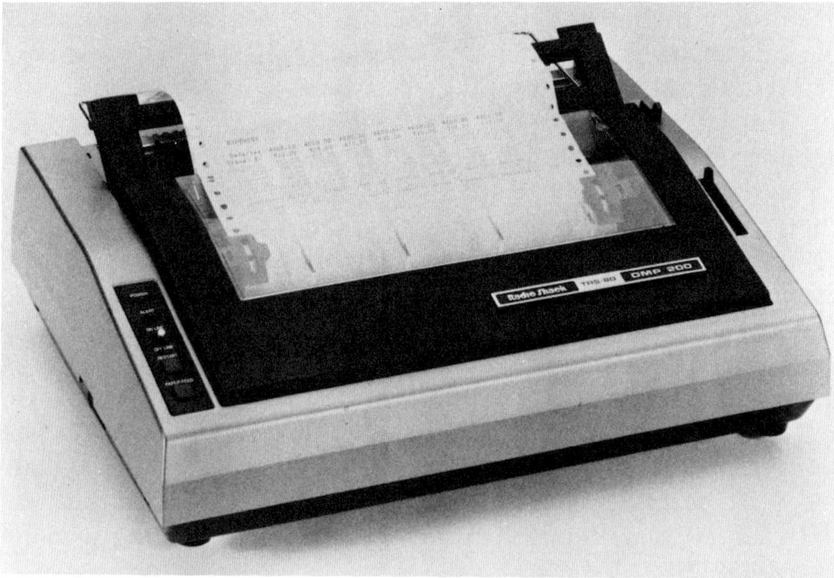

Above: **a Radio Shack dot-matrix printer.**
Below: **the TRS-80 Daisy Wheel Printer.**
Facing page: **a daisy wheel, being held by an International Telephone and Telegraph engineer.**

Qume

The drum printer, the chain or train printer, and the band or belt printer are the principal, high-speed, solid-character printers. They all do a line at a time and are hammer-striking in operation. In each case, the characters spin rapidly behind the ribbon and paper. There are 80 or 132 individual hammers, each one at a print position or spot where a character may appear on the line. The hammers are automatically tripped as the proper characters whiz by. In this way, an entire line can be printed almost at once. These printers can turn out up to 3,000 lines per minute.

Mechanical differences in the way the characters are arranged distinguish these printers from each other. The drum printer has the characters on a spinning cylindrical drum; a complete set of characters rings the surface of the drum at each print point. In the chain printer, perhaps five full sets of characters are mounted on a speeding loop that resembles a bicycle chain. The so-called band printer has several sets of characters on a broad, rapidly rotating belt.

Dot-matrix printers use a rectangular head, or grid, containing from thirty-five to more than a hundred needlelike hammers. They have either one head, or a set of heads with one head at each print position. A pattern of the tiny hammers strikes the ribbon and paper to outline the desired character. The more hammers or dots in the rectangle, the more the dot-matrix letter looks like a solid character.

When there is only one head, the dot matrix functions like a serial printer. But if there is a full set of heads, it can produce an entire line at a time. As with the solid-character printers, the dot-matrix line printer is faster than the dot-matrix serial printer.

NON-IMPACT PRINTERS

As their name indicates, non-impact printers create the characters on paper without striking the paper. The non-impacts work more like copying machines than like typewriters.

Non-impacts have two major advantages over other printers. First, they are much faster. In the impact printer, the paper must stop moving for an instant while the characters are imprinted on it. The contrary is true of non-impact printers. The paper keeps moving while the characters are entered. As a result, the faster non-impact printers can turn out more than 20,000 lines per minute.

An added feature of the non-impact printer is its silent operation. For this reason, most offices prefer the non-impacts over the noisy hammer-striking printers. The rackety impact printers are usually confined to a separate computer room.

One serious handicap of the non-impact printer is its inability to make copies. With an impact printer, up to five copies at a time can be made by placing extra ribbons and paper behind the original. To make multiple copies with a non-impact printer, each copy has to be run through the machine over again or photocopied. Another problem is that many non-impact printers require special, expensive paper.

Non-impact printers come in a few basic designs. Central to many of the latest devices is a laser beam. The exact ways in which the laser works is a carefully kept trade secret.

PLOTTERS

A company president asks for graphs and charts to see state-by-state sales and profit figures. A group of consumer experts are given a pie-shaped diagram showing the amount of tax money spent on nutrition studies. A weather forecaster pores over a map of highs and lows to spot important weather patterns around the country.

Graphs, diagrams, charts, maps, and drawings are examples of graphics produced by computer output devices called *plotters*.

Plotter manufacturers have devised many ways in which to transfer information from the CPU onto paper or another surface.

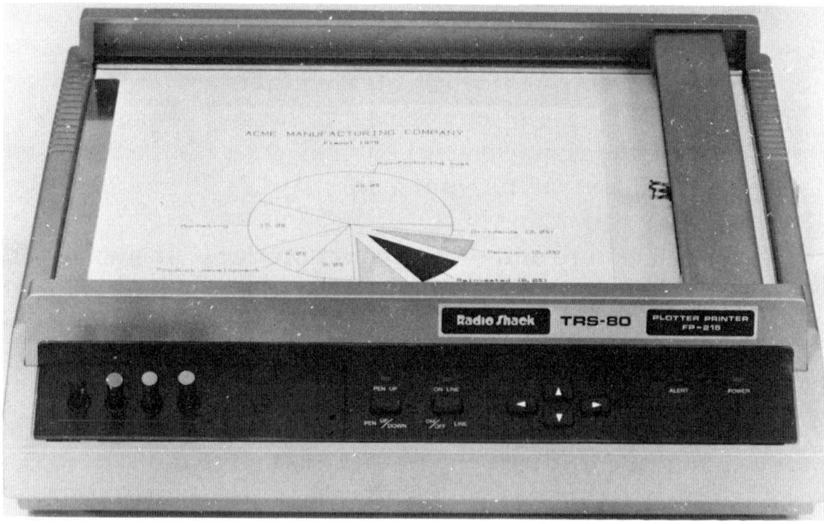
ACME MANUFACTURING COMPANY
Radio Shack
TRS-80
PLOTTER PRINTER
FP-215
PEN UP
ON LINE
ALERT
POWER

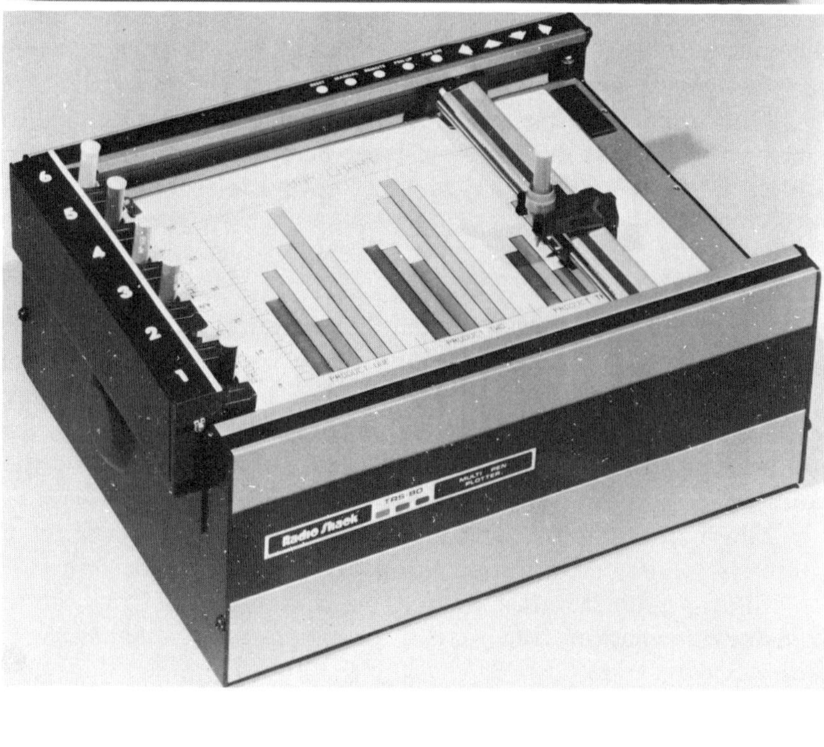
6
5
4
3
2
1
TRS-80
MULTI PEN
PLOTTER
Radio Shack

Some computers direct the plotter to move one or more pens over the paper and thereby draw the graphic representation. Others create electrical charges on the paper wherever lines are to appear. Heat or chemical treatment or a toner then makes the lines visible.

Electric-utility companies frequently use plotters. Often such businesses need to forecast the amount of electricity that will be required over the following months. The long columns of numbers produced as a result of computer calculations are cumbersome to handle and difficult to understand. Therefore, they are often plotted and presented to the user in the form of a line graph.

Before the electric company's graph is plotted, the computer processes all the available data. Figures on customer use of electricity and the weather during the same period a year before are fed into the computer. Any expected increase in the number of customers and the temperature forecast for the following months are also considered.

After processing, the results go to the plotter, which produces charts showing the expected electrical usage. These charts are used to enable the electric company to decide how much fuel to buy. In addition, graphs are often sent to consumers to explain changes in rate.

DISPLAY TERMINALS

Computer output recorded on paper by printers and plotters is called *hard copy*. But what happens when there is no need for

Diagrams, charts, maps, and drawings can all be created using machines called plotters.

hard copy? The travel agent who wants to see the flight times of planes to New York City, the librarian who wants to know whether a certain book is out on loan, the stockbroker who needs to learn the current price of a stock—these workers do not need to have hard copy. In fact, in the situations mentioned, permanent printed records would be wasteful.

Large numbers of users with no use for hard copy turn to their video display terminal. Another name for this output device is *CRT* (cathode-ray tube). The tube looks and works much like your home TV set. But while the cathode-ray, or picture, tube of your TV shows you pictures transmitted from a broadcasting studio, the computer CRT displays computer-created characters and graphics.

Display terminals may be located at some distance, even hundreds of miles away, from the CPU. Nevertheless, CRTs are able to call up a wide assortment of information in various forms from the computer.

Certain advanced CRTs can call up an entire page of data at one time. Perhaps you have seen this system in your library, bank, or school. A coal-mine nurse, for instance, may use paging to call up a list of the names and addresses of all miners who are due for chest X rays.

Suppose a principal wants to compile a list of names of all the students who have birthdays during the summer. He or she may use the "scrolling" feature found on some CRTs. A list of all youngsters in the school slowly moves up the screen as the principal searches for all those with birthdays during July or August.

This video display terminal is being used by an engineer to make corrections in a product design.

IBM

Reverse video is another popular aspect of the more expensive CRTs. With reverse video it is possible to show either dark characters on a light background or light characters on a dark background. In some advanced models the user can even reverse just one part of the screen.

A certain store owner displays all his accounts this way. With reverse-video highlighting, he can quickly separate out those who do not pay their bills on time from those who do.

CRTs frequently answer users' questions based on data stored in the computer. This is known as *transaction-oriented processing*.

Let's say a hotel-chain clerk wants to know if there is a single room available in the chain's Atlanta hotel. On a keyboard connected to the CRT the clerk types in the inquiry. The terminal displays the answer in seconds. In a similar way, at the end of each day, a bank manager asks the bank's computer to display the total amount of money deposited between nine and three o'clock. The president of an auto company asks how many cars were sold during the previous month.

Sometimes the computer may follow up by asking the user questions of its own. Suppose the computer shows that an auto company's dealers sold a total of 23,000 cars in 1983. The computer might then ask the company's executive in words spelled out on the screen: Do you want to see the number sold by each dealer? The president is instructed to press either Y (for Yes) to get those figures or N (for No) if not interested.

In the next step, the computer may ask: Do you want to see the names and addresses of those who made the highest sales? Press Y or N.

Finally, if a printer is attached to the display terminal, the CRT may ask: Do you want a printed copy of this information? Press Y or N.

There are output devices to suit every need and purpose. Can you recall some that you have seen? What purposes did they serve?

CHAPTER SIX

COMPUTER PROGRAMMING

Bring shoes to shoemaker.
Withdraw money from bank.
Buy hot dogs if on sale.
Order meat for hamburgers.
Make party decorations.

This is one person's list of errands to run on a Saturday morning. It is a sequence of instructions on what must be done to achieve certain results. In this case, the results are to have the right shoes, money, food, and decorations for a planned party.

A computer program is likewise a list of steps the computer must follow in order to solve a problem or perform a certain task. Even the best, biggest, and most advanced computer can do nothing until it gets very detailed orders on every action it must take. For the computer (the hardware) to work, it must have a program (software) to direct it.

THE PROGRAMMER/ANALYST

The job of preparing computer programs is usually performed by experts known as *programmer/analysts*. The word *analyst* is used because the programmer is trained to examine, or analyze, the many ways the computer can be used to solve a given problem.

The first question analysts ask themselves is: What sort of information or action do I want from the computer? Then they ask: What sort of data is available, and can it be entered into the computer's memory? And finally: How should the computer process the data to provide the desired results?

Once this analysis is complete, the programming part of the work begins. The program, a list of carefully worded, step-by-step instructions, is entered by the programmer into the computer. This enables the computer to complete the required task.

Let's imagine that you have the job of programmer/analyst. Here is a simple sort of problem you might have to solve: A restaurant owner wants her computer to calculate the pay for each of her employees, based on the number of hours worked and the rate of pay per hour. From this gross pay, she then wants to deduct taxes, insurance, and union dues. Further, she would like the computer to prepare the actual checks and produce a summary of the total payroll.

FLOWCHART

Your first act in planning such a program would be to construct a diagram called a *flowchart*. Using a pencil and paper, you would write out all the separate steps needed to meet the restaurant owner's needs. You would then arrange those steps in a strictly logical order.

Computer programmers use a number of standard symbols in making up a flowchart. Here are a few of the principal ones:

The start or finish of a program.

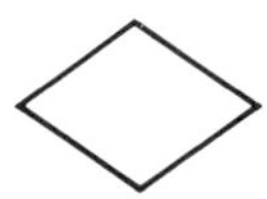

A decision with a yes or no answer.

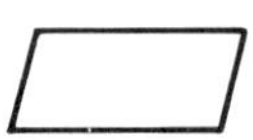

Input or output; either write or read information.

A processing operation, such as calculating.

On page 56 is the flowchart you might prepare for the restaurant payroll.

COMPUTER LANGUAGES

Once you have finished and checked the flowchart, the next step is to enter the program into the main storage of the computer. In the early days of computers, to do this you had to use the language the computer understood. Just as you cannot communicate with a Russian-speaking person unless you speak Russian, so you could not communicate with a computer unless you used so-called *machine language.*

But machine-language instructions are seldom used today. Writing a program in machine language is slow and difficult. Also, each computer has a different code or format of machine-language instructions. The instructions for one computer will not run on another. Further, errors are easy to make and hard to locate when a computer is programmed this way.

So-called *assembler languages* began to replace machine-language instructions around 1950. These languages use the assembler program in the computer to change a code representing human language into machine language. In this system, a code of up to three hundred symbols represents the various computer operations. As an example, in one assembler language, MC means "move a character," AC means "add one character to another," SC means "subtract one character from another," and so on. Each time the programmer types in a few characters, the assembler language instructs the computer to translate them into machine language.

Assembler language, though an improvement over machine language, still has its difficulties. It can be used only on a particular computer, and every single step has to be spelled out. An easier approach to computer programming is by means of the so-called *high-level languages.*

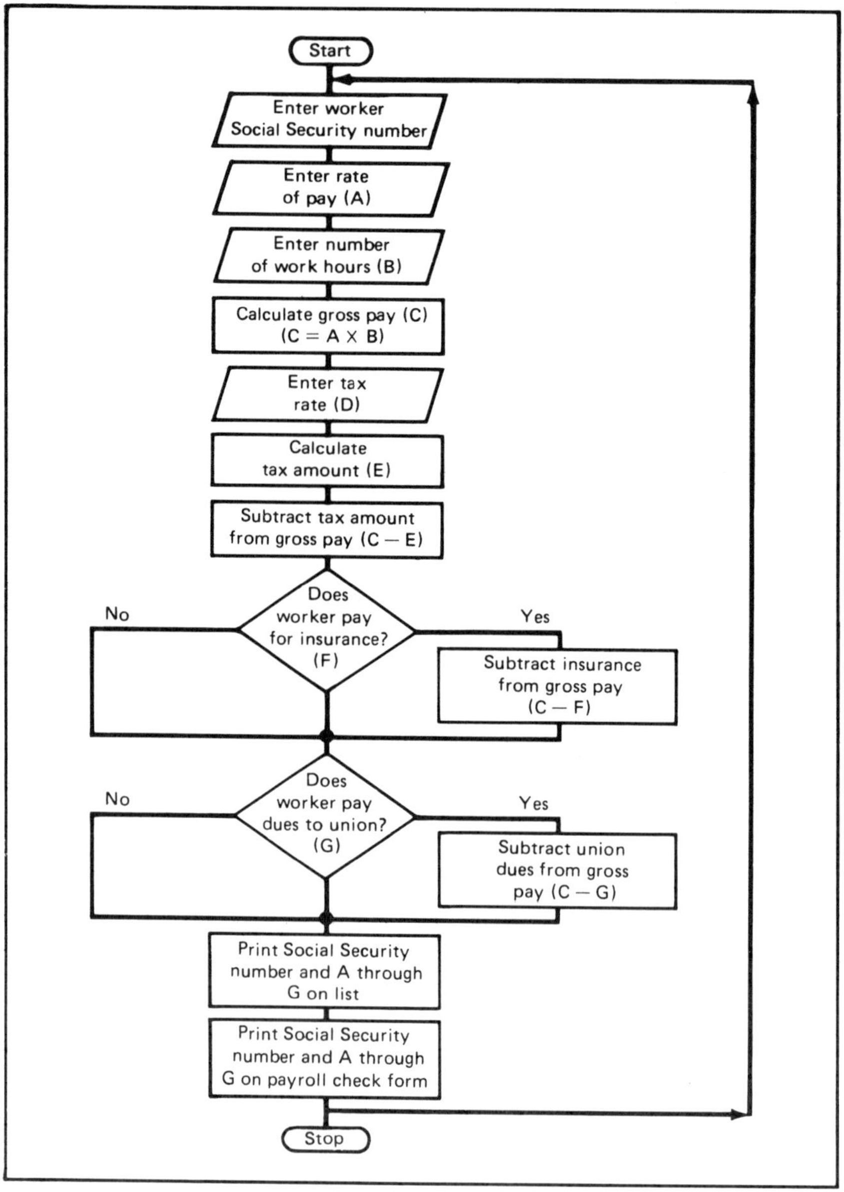
Start
Enter worker Social Security number
Enter rate of pay (A)
Enter number of work hours (B)
Calculate gross pay (C) (C = A × B)
Enter tax rate (D)
Calculate tax amount (E)
Subtract tax amount from gross pay (C — E)
Does worker pay for insurance? (F)
No
Yes
Subtract insurance from gross pay (C — F)
Does worker pay dues to union? (G)
No
Yes
Subtract union dues from gross pay (C — G)
Print Social Security number and A through G on list
Print Social Security number and A through G on payroll check form
Stop

It may surprise you to learn that there are hundreds of high-level languages. Many are known by acronyms of their names. Among the most popular are FORTRAN (FORmula TRANslator), COBOL (COmmon Business-Oriented Language), BASIC (Beginners All-purpose Symbolic Instruction Code), APL (A Programming Language), and PL/1 (Program Language No. 1).

All high-level languages have two things in common. First, they can all be used on more than one computer. Second, they all make it possible to accomplish several operations with a single instruction.

Suppose you own a business, and you want a summary of all your customers—where they live, how much business they did with you last year, and so on. Their names, addresses, and purchase totals are already in your computer's memory. In the earlier languages, your instructions might involve several steps: READ THE NAME, READ THE ADDRESS, READ THE PURCHASES, and so on. With a high-level language, it is usually possible to achieve the same result with a single command: READ THE FILE.

Let's get back now to the illustration of preparing a restaurant-payroll program by computer. This is what the instructions might look like written in FORTRAN:

```
READ, NUMB, HRS, PARA
```

In words, this *source statement*, as it is called, instructs the computer to read the worker's Social Security number (NUMB) the number of hours worked (HRS), and the rate of pay (PARA).

```
GRPA = HRS * PARA
```

Gross pay (GRPA) is equal to hours worked multiplied by (*) the pay rate.

```
WRITE NUMB, GRPA
```

Write the worker's Social Security number and gross pay.

Other computer languages, of course, have different symbols and formats. But no matter which one is used, the approach is very much the same.

AFTER PROGRAMMING

A computer does *only* what it is instructed to do. Even the best computer does not show any cleverness or common sense. Therefore, the slightest error in the program, such as the omission of one minor step or the failure to include one possible outcome, will cause the program not to work.

That is why there must always be a test of the program before it is run. Computer experts say that this is the time "to get the bugs out." The testing of the program is known as *debugging.* The name refers to the early days when computers were huge assemblies of warm vacuum tubes set in open cabinets. Bugs and mice would indeed get into the computer and cause it to malfunction. Debugging, then, literally meant making sure that no insect or rodent had damaged some part of the machine. Although this is no longer a common danger, the term hangs on.

The programmer sometimes debugs the program by first running a prepackaged test program and checking the results. Sometimes the same data is run with the new program as well as with a standard program. The results are then compared.

It is rare indeed for a new program to go smoothly and without error. Almost always several bugs do show up. Then the programmer has to review the program, locate the trouble spots, and make the necessary corrections.

Often the mistakes seem to be minor and unimportant—the programmer omitted the decimal point when indicating a sum of

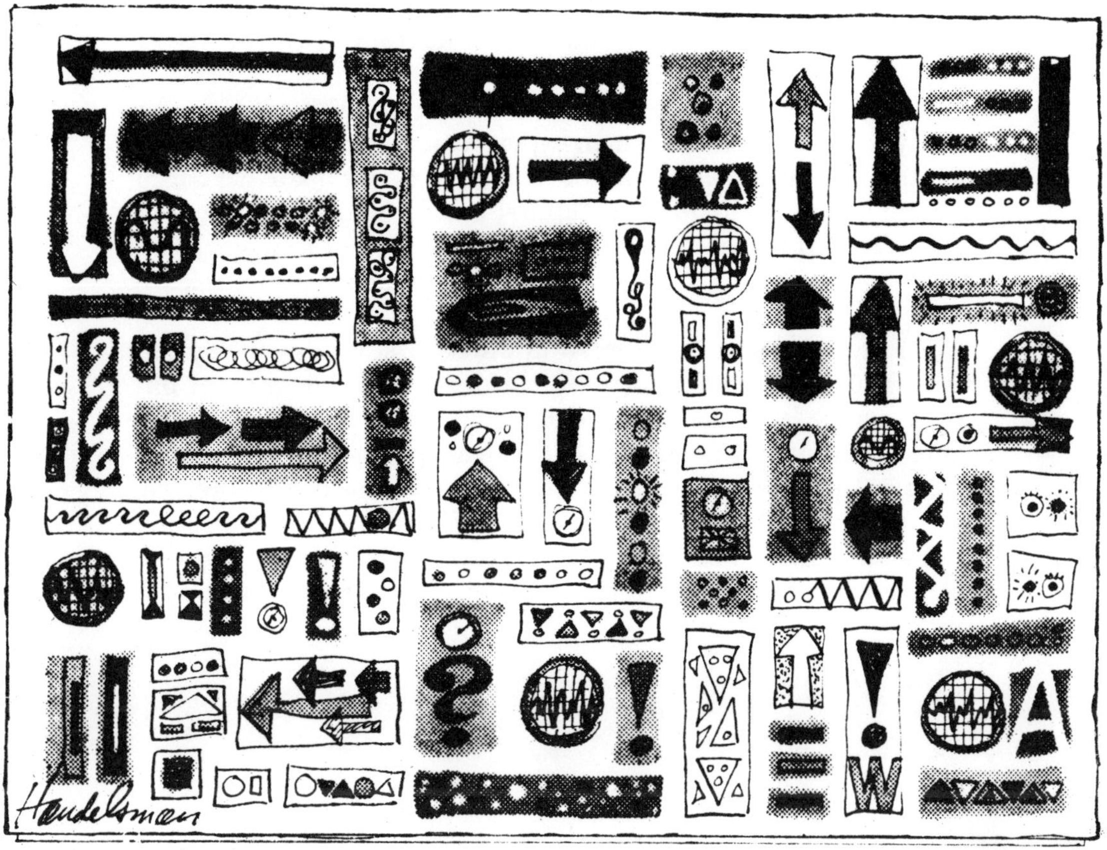

"True, but I dare say
you and I are only as good
as the data fed into us."

money, or the computer was instructed on what to do when figure A is larger than B and when A is smaller than B but ignored the possibility that A might be equal to B. Mistakes like these can completely ruin a computer program if not caught during debugging.

Once all the bugs are out of the program, the processing is ready to begin. Quite often an expert is not even needed to operate the computer. All it takes is someone to enter the data accurately. The rest is up to the computer and program. And the problem is solved faster, more accurately, with greater reliability, and at lower cost than a human being working at the same task.

The computer has already revolutionized the way people gather facts and turn them into useful information. Government officials, scientists, business executives, and many others are now able to process vast quantities of data at speeds that were impossible before the introduction of computer data processing. The results—more accurate record keeping, better decision-making, remarkable new discoveries, improved services—have not only accrued to the users of the processed data but to every one of us.

GLOSSARY

Address. The place in the computer where data or instructions are stored.

Assembler language. A computer language in which the computer translates various code symbols into a form the machine can understand.

Binary. The number system used by computers; it employs only two digits, 0 and 1. These represent power off and power on (or low power and high power).

Bit. The basic unit of data a computer can handle; each bit is either a zero (0) or a one (1). These represent power off and power on.

Bug. A defect in a computer program. Debugging is the process of getting rid of any bugs.

Byte. A group of eight bits, which together represent a character such as a number or letter.

Central processing unit (CPU). The main processing part of the computer to which all other parts are connected.

Character. Any digit, letter, punctuation mark, or symbol.

Computer. An electronic device that carries out mathematical and logical operations at high speeds.

CRT. A cathode-ray tube; this TV-screenlike device displays computer data being entered and computer output. It is usually connected to a computer keyboard. Also called *video display screen.*

Data. Facts and figures. Plural of *datum,* but is also used in the singular to represent the collective noun *information.*

Data processing. The handling of words and numbers by a computer to obtain useful information.

Diskette. A small, magnetized disk for storing data in the form of tiny magnetic spots. Also called *floppy disk.*

Field. A set of one or more characters that make up a complete, but single, unit of data. A person's Social Security number, for example, has a "field" of nine characters.

Floppy disk. See *Diskette.*

Flowchart. A fully labeled diagram showing the various steps of a computer program.

Hardware. The mechanical parts of a computer system; the machine itself.

High-level language. One of the modern computer languages, such as BASIC, FORTRAN, COBOL, and PASCAL, in which commonly used words represent a number of related computer operations.

Input. Data entered into a computer.

Input device. Any device that receives data and introduces it into a computer. A keyboard is a common input device.

Keyboard. A typewriter-like device with letters, numbers, and symbols arranged for entering data into a computer.

Keypunch. A device for coding data by punching a pattern of holes in stiff paper cards. Rarely used any more.

Key-to-disk. A device for coding data by creating magnetic spots on a magnetized disk.

Key-to-tape. A device for coding data by creating magnetic spots on a reel of magnetized tape.

Machine language. The language the computer understands. Information is coded into the binary system (see *Binary*) by assembler programs (see *Assembler language*) to translate it into machine-readable form.

Magnetic-core storage. A kind of computer storage where data is located on a grid of tiny magnetized metal rings called *cores.*

Magnetic disk. A form of computer storage in which data is stored as magnetic spots on a hard or flexible flat disk or platter.

Magnetic tape. A form of computer storage in which data is stored as tiny magnetic spots on a reel of magnetized tape.

Mainframe. Any one of the largest computers. Also called *maxicomputers.*

Memory. See *Storage.*

Microcomputer. A desktop computer, usually consisting of a keyboard, a disk drive, and a video display screen. Also called a *small, personal,* or *home computer.*

Microprocessor. An entire central processing unit with semiconductors and transistors etched onto the surface of a small silicon chip.

Minicomputer. A computer of medium size and power.

Output. Information produced by a computer.

Output device. A device, such as a printer, plotter, or video display screen, that sends processed information from inside the computer to the outside.

Plotter. An output device that produces graphic representations, such as charts, maps, graphs, or drawings.

Printer. An output device that prints characters on paper.

Program. Instructions given to a computer to solve a problem or accomplish a task.

Punched cards. Stiff paper cards with holes used to enter data into a computer.

Software. The programs that direct the operation of a computer.

Storage. The part of a computer that can store, or remember, data or instructions. Also called *memory.* A computer has a main storage (internal) and auxiliary storage (external).

Terminal. A device used for entering data into a computer and getting useful information out; usually made up of a keyboard and a video display screen.

Time-sharing. A means by which several or many people use the processing capabilities and huge storage of a large computer at virtually the same time.

Video display screen. See *CRT.*

Word processing. The manipulation of text or documents on a computer.

INDEX